S0-APM-050

F1rst Guide for the College Placement Test (CPT)

F1rst Guide for the College Placement Test (CPT)

✦

A quality educational guide & review for the college entry-level placement test.

Rachel Goldberg, M.Ed.

iUniverse, Inc.

New York Lincoln Shanghai

F1rst Guide for the College Placement Test (CPT)
A quality educational guide & review for the college entry-level placement test.

Copyright © 2007 by Rachel Goldberg

All rights reserved. No part of this book may be used or reproduced by any means, graphic, electronic, or mechanical, including photocopying, recording, taping or by any information storage retrieval system without the written permission of the publisher except in the case of brief quotations embodied in critical articles and reviews.

iUniverse books may be ordered through booksellers or by contacting:

iUniverse
2021 Pine Lake Road, Suite 100
Lincoln, NE 68512
www.iuniverse.com
1-800-Authors (1-800-288-4677)

Because of the dynamic nature of the Internet, any Web addresses or links contained in this book may have changed since publication and may no longer be valid.

The views expressed in this work are solely those of the author and do not necessarily reflect the views of the publisher, and the publisher hereby disclaims any responsibility for them.

ISBN: 978-0-595-45652-9 (pbk)
ISBN: 978-0-595-89954-8 (ebk)

Printed in the United States of America

Only perfect practice makes perfect.

—Vince Lombardi

To M.E.E.

The good news about the CPT:
the test is usually FREE or cheap!

The better news: you can take the test multiple times (3)!

The even better news: there's <u>no</u> time limit!

Contents

PART I—CPT OVERVIEW

CPT OVERVIEW

Placement testing is mandated by many community colleges for students who are either a) degree seeking and/or b) enrolling in college-level English or math. Often other standardized and achievement tests (i.e. ACT®/SAT®) are sufficient for the school and students will not be required to take the computerized placement test. Some programs do not accept any CPT exemptions and students will be required to take the computerized placement test regardless of previous tests completed.

The CPT is not timed. All questions are multiple choice except the essay. Each section contains about 20 questions and will take you 20-50 minutes to complete. Approximate/ average time for completing all sections of the test is 2 to 2 ½ hours.

Note: You are <u>not allowed</u> to cheat, use dictionaries, calculators, notebooks, or textbooks of any kind on the CPT. Scratch paper for the test will be provided by your testing center. Following the test period, no test materials or notes may be removed from the testing room.

You may leave your testing session at any time in instances like an illness, a personal matter or an appointment. Verify all situations with your testing center. You can return to complete the testing any time within five workdays. When you recommence the test, you will begin at the exact point at which you left.

The College Board developed the ACCUPLACER® Computerized College Placement Tests (CPTs).

Every school in America is different. <u>Check with your school to identify your school's specific passing scores.</u>

Ask as many relevant questions as possible prior to taking the CPT at *your school* to ensure you have a full understanding of testing procedures.

Suggested questions may include:

- Does the school offer free test prep classes?

- Are there any available sample tests for students?

- Where and when is the test?

The CPT is computerized but no special computer skills are required to complete the test. You will use either the keyboard or the mouse to enter your answers, write your essay, and supply personal identification information. Having scrap paper and pencils next to the computer will aide you in writing any notes or problems while working on the screen. (According to The College Board ACCUPLACER® there are eight multiple choice computerized placement tests available in the ACCUPLACER® program as well as two different writing tests for which you write an essay.) *Your college will determine which of these tests you should take.* The scores from these computerized placement tests will help determine what English, mathematics, and reading courses are most appropriate for you at this time.

The questions on the CPT appear one at a time on the computer screen and most questions are multiple choice. Once you have answered a particular question you *cannot* return to that question.

Each test is adaptive and tries to work within your zone of proximal development. This means the computer automatically determines the question(s) presented to you based on the responses on prior questions. The computer then selects the next question(s) to ask without being too easy or too difficult in an attempt to determine your current academic level.

The scores obtained from the CPT are used for *placement purposes.* The purpose of the CPT is for you to take a brief placement test and provide a score to your school to determine your readiness for college-level courses in English, reading, and/or mathematics. Your scores will most likely determine in what core classes you are to be placed. Essentially, the higher the score, the more likely you will be placed in a higher level class, the lower the score, the lower the level of your class placement. Regardless of the score outcome, you will be geared to the level course best suited to your educational needs as directed by both the CPT and your particular academic institution.

Fear not, this test is not going to make or break you; this is most likely just the beginning of your journey as a college student. Whether starting out in remedial classes or higher level courses *you can be successful.*

You must complete the CPT before matriculation. Assessment precedes the registration process. Your level of academic performance will be reviewed and on file prior to being placed or placing one's self into a class. Depending on your CPT scores and your school guidelines you may be placed in college level classes or preparatory classes.

Depending on your score you *may need to take required prep classes prior to taking the college required courses* such as Basic Math, Intro to Algebra, and/or English Communications.

These non-credit prep classes prepare you for the material in the more advanced credit bearing classes. Beware: *The prep classes don't typically count for actual college credit toward a degree and they still cost money.* The prep classes are intended to get you to the level(s) you need to be in order to learn your core college curriculum and excel in higher education.

How you find out about your scores depends on how your college has set up the testing. When you have completed the tests, you may see a report of your scores on the screen and you may receive a printed report of your scores. Your scores can only be obtained through your college and not The College Board.

Retesting schedules vary by school; often, you may take the first retest after 24 hours, and other times you may have to wait a month. Then, after your *first retest,* you may retest again every 30 days. Reasons for retesting may include dissatisfaction with the initial test score and/or a desire to improve scores after taking remedial classes.

Remember to bring a photo ID with you when you go to test. Appointments are not typically necessary, testing site hours are usually posted and convenient; make sure you give yourself ample time prior to testing site closing time.

When sitting down to take your test you will be asked to enter personal background information such as Social Security number, name and address. Then, the first page of the first test you are taking and a sample question will appear. Once you are ready to move on, you will begin the actual test. Each page presents a question and several possible answer choices. According to The College Board "the page may also include additional information that is needed to answer the question such as a reading passage, picture or table of information."

The number of questions on each test section ranges from 12 to 20 questions.

Once you have *verified* your answer, you cannot return to that question.

If you opt to retake the CPT you will be presented with a different set of questions than presented in the previous testing session.

Test scores are only one common way to measure skills. In order to achieve a clearer picture of your abilities and potential, you should review your scores, past academic achievements, and nontraditional experiences to get a full personal portrait. If you believe you should be allowed to enroll in a higher-level class than recommended because your math/ English/writing skills are better than your test scores indicate, please contact your school counselor, administrator or someone who is capable of determining your class schedule and making significant academic decisions. Just a note though, chances are you need the remediation, the tests are accurate under normal circumstances and prevent students from taking classes that are too difficult and for which they are unprepared.

Being under-prepared or "rusty" in a skill area like reading, writing, or mathematics is a common problem, especially for students returning to school after a hiatus. It may be useful to participate in brief review classes, study groups, training or lab classes, tutoring sessions or bookstore visits to brush up on once learned skills.

Several options to assist in best preparing for the CPT include:

Look through and use new or used textbooks in the specific areas of interest. For example, review a used pre-algebra textbook from your child, neighbor, college bookstore, etc.

Perform practice problems. Make sure to review the answers.

Several *computer software programs* are available on varying academic skills and levels, feel free to indulge your brain and use one. They can also be fun!

Make sure you've had your eyes checked recently to ensure you are not having vision difficulties, especially while studying or test taking.

Talk to a local librarian, and visit the *public library*. The library offers a wealth of information and resources, including test-taking software and computers. If you don't already have a public library card, go get one now.

Complete several (more) *practice tests* and review answers to determine errors and make corrections. Learn about your mistakes so you will avoid repeating them.

If I were to recommend one academic publisher for teaching/reviewing skills, especially in math, it would be *Saxon Publishers*, A Harcourt Achieve Imprint; you can find them on the web.

According to The College Board, your test scores and the information you provide when taking the tests will only be provided to The College Board™, the college at which you are taking the tests or enrolled, and to the state. The information may be used for counseling, advisement and placement purposes and may be used to document whether or not you have met state testing requirements. The College Board™ states they may also use it for research and training purposes but your test information will not be disclosed for any other purpose without your permission.

PART II—ABOUT THE CPT SUBTESTS

ARITHMETIC

The arithmetic test measures your skills in three main categories.

1. Operations with <u>whole numbers</u> and <u>fractions</u>

   - Addition, subtraction, multiplication, division
   - Recognizing equivalent fractions and mixed numbers

2. Operations with <u>decimals</u> and <u>percents</u>

   - Addition, subtraction, multiplication, and division
   - Percent problems, decimal recognition, fraction and percent equivalences, and estimation problems

3. Applications and problem solving

   - <u>Rate</u>, <u>percent</u>, and <u>measurement</u> problems
   - <u>Geometry</u> problems
   - Distribution of a quantity into its fractional parts

ELEMENTARY ALGEBRA

The elementary algebra test measures your skills in three main areas.

1. Operations with <u>integers</u> and <u>rational numbers</u>

   - Includes computation with integers and negative rationales

   - Use of <u>absolute values</u> and ordering

2. Operations with <u>algebraic expressions</u>

   - Simple formulas and expressions

   - Adding, subtracting, multiplying and dividing <u>monomials</u> and <u>polynomials</u>

   - Evaluating positive <u>rational roots</u> and <u>exponents</u>

   - <u>Simplifying algebraic fractions</u> and <u>factoring</u>

3. Solving <u>equations</u>, <u>inequalities</u>, and <u>word problems</u>

   - Include solving systems of <u>linear equations</u>

   - <u>Quadratic equations</u> by factoring

   - <u>Geometric reasoning</u>

   - Translation of written phrases into algebraic expressions and <u>graphing</u>

COLLEGE LEVEL MATHEMATICS

The test measures your proficiency from intermediate algebra through pre-calculus.

1. Algebraic operations

   - Simplify rational algebraic expressions
   - Factoring
   - Expanding polynomials
   - Work with roots and exponents

2. Solutions of equations and inequalities

   - Linear and quadratic

3. Coordinate geometry

   - Plane and coordinate geometry
   - Straight line
   - Conics
   - Sets of points
   - Graphing functions

4. Application and algebraic topics

   - Complex numbers
   - Series and sequences

- Determinants
- Permutations and combinations

5. Functions and trigonometry

- Polynomials
- Algebraic, exponential, logarithmic and trigonometric functions

Math sample questions are not provided here. Practice problems can be found through numerous outlets, including several of the websites listed at the end of this guide, countless math oriented textbooks/workbooks and other preparatory college math exam books. After using this guide as a preparatory tool, please refer to these resources for practicing and enhancing your math skills.

SENTENCE SKILLS TEST

The sentence skills test measures your understanding of sentence structure, how sentences are put together and what makes a sentence complete and clear.

Logic
Complete sentence structure
Meaning and organization

Questions will ask you to select the <u>best version</u> of the underlined part of the sentence. Choose the best word or phrase that most closely resembles and replaces the underlined portion. The first option will be the same as the original sentence and then three additional choices will be given; if the original sentence is the best version you will select the first option. Questions will also ask you to <u>rewrite</u> a sentence making sure it has the same meaning as the original sentence given.

TIPS

Read the questions to yourself to <u>hear</u> which sentence choice "sounds" right. Usually, you can <u>hear</u> what the correct answer should be.

If you become confused at any point, take a break from the questions. Since you cannot go ahead and return to questions, just stop working for a minute, day dream for a moment to relax yourself and then return to the question at hand.

Use the process of elimination to eliminate certain answers and narrow your choices.

College is about using <u>proper </u>English, not slang, not TV talk. Focus on mastering the English language and avoid using mispronunciations, poor sentence structure, and slang.

Four Sentence Sample Questions

Select the best version of the underlined part of the sentence. The first choice is the same as the original sentence. If you think the original sentence is best, choose the first answer.

1. <u>To fly, take the train and driving</u> are the best ways to travel from Miami to New York.

    a. To fly, take the train and driving

    b. To fly, to take the train and to drive

    c. Flying, to take the train and driving

    d. Flying, taking the train and driving

(Correct answer is d)

2. <u>After me graduate</u> college I plan on being a newscaster.

    a. After me graduate

    b. After we graduate

    c. After me graduating

    d. After I graduate

(Correct answer d)

Rewrite the sentence below following the directions given. Keep in mind your new sentence should be well written and should have essentially the same meaning as the sentence given.

3. *Erica's wedding day turned out to be beautiful once the rain stopped and sun appeared.*

Rewrite beginning with

<u>Once the rain stopped</u>

The next words will be

a. and the sun appeared

b. Erica's wedding turned

c. and the wedding day turned

d. the wedding became beautiful

(Correct answer a)

4. *Because she was the first woman on the moon, she became a historical celebrity.*

Rewrite the sentence, beginning with

<u>She became</u>

The next words will be

a. the first woman on

b. the moon

c. a historical woman

d. a historical celebrity

(Correct answer d)

READING COMPREHENSION TEST

This test measures your ability to understand and grasp what you read.

Answer the questions on the basis of what is stated or implied in the passage.

1. Questions will ask you to read the statement/passage and then choose the best answer to the question.

2. Other reading comprehension questions will offer two underlined sentences followed by a specific question or statement. You are to read the two sentences, and then choose the best answer to satisfy the question posed.

TIPS

Make sure your answer makes sense.

If you don't think a particular answer option is correct, you're probably right, stick with your intuition.

Use the process of elimination as you always should with multiple choice questions; pick one of the remaining choices.

Pretend you needed to make a rational argument defending why your answer was the right one versus the other options; if you can support your choice you will be more likely to have selected the correct answer.

Two reading comprehension sample questions

Read the statement/passage and choose the best answer to the question.

1. While traveling by airplane both domestically and internationally there have been many new rules put in place requiring individuals and their luggage to meet certain requirements. Examples of these rules include the enforcement of size and weight for on-board luggage. Additionally, the number of items allowed on the plane is also occasionally enforced.

   The main idea of the paragraph is about

   a. the hassle of traveling by airplane

   b. Different means of transportation

   c. Rules implemented while traveling by plane

   d. How many items are allowed to be transported by plane

   (Correct answer c)

2. <u>Major corporations in America value their employees and the needs of their employees. Any American corporation with over 15 employees offers each employee 10 sick</u>

NWTC Library
2740 W. Mason St.
Green Bay, WI 54307

days, 1 month maternity leave and 3 personal days per year.

What does the second sentence do?

a. It contradicts the first sentence

b. It reinforces the first sentence

c. It provides the main idea

d. It draws a well delineated conclusion

(Correct answer b)

WRITING TEST

-Typically there are two writing test offered: one for native English speakers and the other for non-native English speakers

-You will be given a topic and asked to write an essay

-Plan, write, review, and revise your essay

-Your score is based on the overall quality of your writing

The purpose of the essay question is to *write as strong of an essay as possible;* do not be concerned if you do not believe genuinely or profoundly in what you are writing; focus on getting the best score possible.

TIPS to writing the <u>best</u> answer on the essay question.

1. *Write a 5 paragraph* essay.

> The *first paragraph is an introduction* to your point.

> The *last paragraph is going to wrap up (conclude)* your point.

> The *middle three paragraphs* are examples *supporting* your point;

use only *one example per paragraph.*

2. Each paragraph must be at least 3 sentences.

3. Proofread your essay at least once to make sure it is coherent, words are spelled correctly, and punctuation is taken into consideration.

Following is a sample essay subject/question.

(Use the TIPS provided to write the best 5 paragraph essay possible!)

Viva High School requires each high school student to participate in a physical education class every semester of their four years of high school. State law only requires a high school student to have one semester of physical education. Some parents, teachers, and students think Viva's school requirements are unfair and overly demanding.

Write an essay expressing your point of view in which you take a position either for or against Viva's physical education requirements. Be sure to defend your position with logical arguments and appropriate examples.

(You may want to use a separate sheet of paper and/or practice on your computer.)

PART III—MORE WAYS TO EARN HIGHER SCORES

DO THIS NOW & ALWAYS:

-Often times, standardized and achievement tests offer sample questions, let the sample questions act as a focusing tool, not as a hindrance.

-Use *the process of elimination* to cross off the choices you know are incorrect and narrow down the possibilities for the correct choice.

-Go with your first choice if you get muddled.

-Remember school is fun and its purpose is to educate, challenge, and offer and open new opportunities.

-A test is just a test. Prepare, ask for assistance when necessary, and put forth effort during this test and all tests.

-Proctors, teachers and aides are hired to help students. Do not be intimidated by authority, you are entitled to ask relevant questions.

-You are entitled to a quiet learning environment and testing environment, do not settle for anything less.

- Write on scrap paper, write on tests underline, highlight, circle, etc. These markings will help determine correct answers, the markings will also keep you on track, and help you easily identify relevant information.

-Practice your English skills by reading often, i.e. newspaper, comics, Sports Illustrated, signs, posters, etc.

-Complete at least one math problem a day—this can be taken from a textbook or workbook. Challenge yourself daily.

RESOURCES & PLACES FOR PRACTICE QUESTIONS

1) http://admin.sfcc.edu/~acres/assess/cptprep.pdf

2) http://www.arapahoe.edu/studentsvcs/testing/placement.html

3) http://asc.ucok.edu/placement_tests.htm

4) www.brevardcc.edu

5) http://www.cerritos.edu/reading/tutorials.htm

6) www.collegeboard.com

7) http://www.collegeboard.com/student/testing/accuplacer/

8) http://cpts.accuplacer.com/docs/StudentGuide.html#_Toc19497949

9) www.fiu.edu

10) http://www.fkcc.edu

11) http://frontrange.edu/FRCCTemplates/FRCC7.aspx?id=1195

12) http://ghc.ctc.edu/counseling/accuplacer.htm

13) http://ghc.ctc.edu/counseling/reading.htm

14) http://www.lscc.edu/admissions/FLCELPT.pdf

15) http://www.mathmax.com/introalg/index.html

16) http://www.mdc.edu/clast/FreeResources.asp#CPT

17) http://www.mymathtest.com

18) http://www.onlinecollegeprep.com

19) http://owl.english.purdue.edu

20) http://www.phx.devry.edu/academics/test_center/placement_tests.asp

21) http://www.spjc.edu/webcentral/admit/place1.htm

22) http://testingoffice.msu.edu/prep.htm

23) http://ucl.broward.edu/guides/cpt.htm

24) http://www.valenciacc.edu/assessments/cpt/cptlnks.cfm

25) http://www.ct4me.net/math_resources.htm

978-0-595-45652-9
0-595-45652-9

6349059R0

Made in the USA
Lexington, KY
12 August 2010